ZERO-BASED BUDGETING TO ZERO-BASED EVERYTHING

A BUSINESS GUIDE TO AUGMENTING ZERO-BASED BUDGETING TO ACHIEVE A STEP-CHANGE IN PERFORMANCE

AUTHOR

Sam Schreim

ISBN: 9781674618005

ABOUT THE AUTHOR

Sam Schreim is the author of the Management Tools Beyond 2020 Series and the founder of Business Model Hackers.

For more information:
www.bmhackers.com
sam@bmhackers.com

FOREWORD

Zero-Based Budgeting (ZBB) is making a comeback and has made it to the top of the list of most adopted management tools among executives in leading global organizations.

As we enter an unprecedented era of economic unpredictability, disruptive technologies, globalization and fierce competition, companies are increasingly finding themselves in search of money to invest in new initiatives which have caused a resurgence in ZBB as a tool of choice among executives.

The last time anyone wrote about the subject was in the 1970s. Does this method still hold ground? Are companies using ZBB in the same manner they used to as in the '70s? Not exactly. Companies that are simply joining the herd and inappropriately adopting the approach as a one-time fix and a cost-cutting tool are disrupting and crippling operations while facing a huge internal backlash.

ZBB is a way of life! What was once used as a scary cost-cutting tool in the '70s has now been revamped as a framework for replacing the once-a-year budgeting process with continuous business monitoring, with ZBB being adopted to drive efficiency and reallocate resources to unleash hidden values and fuel growth. Companies are seizing this opportunity and are adopting the zero-based method to rethink the status quo.

This book covers the entire spectrum of the "Zero-Based" approach and illustrates how ZBB is being adopted not as a one-time fix but as an integrated change management tool that optimizes usage of resources across the value chain and instills accountability for cost across the entire organization.

Adopting ZBB is a cultural shift and requires the adoption of "Zero-Based Thinking" across the organization. You should buy this book whether you are contemplating reinventing your existing budgeting process or you are already working on a ZBB initiative and need to make sure you are on the right track. If you've never heard of ZBB, you should buy this book as the cost of not knowing is not zero-based.

Table Of Contents

INTRODUCTION

Zero-based budgeting is an old technique that's being revived across the business world, to huge success. In this book, not only will you learn what this technique is, but you'll learn where it came from, its benefits, its common pitfalls, and how to implement it into your business. You will also learn how digital technology can be used to augment the zero-based process and how to use digital transformation to create a virtuous cycle of investment. Once you've mastered the zero-based technique in your business' budget, this book will help you to apply this principle across your business plan and foster a zero-based culture of management success. The zero-based principle can be applied to any business, any industry, and any management tool. If you're ready to learn how, simply read on.

Too many businesses get bogged down with unnecessary expenses, excessive amounts of debt, or are gutted by unexpected costs. Worse, efforts to improve business budgeting are often complicated, unrealistic, and, ultimately, funnel money into questionable loans or investment schemes. Financial models for businesses are blanket models based on averages and statistics, and those don't necessarily reflect the specific costs of running your company. The zero-based technique was developed as a simple method to solve all of these problems. Zero-based budgeting provides you with the tools to create a budget based entirely on your company's costs, savings, investments, and financial history. It doesn't use data, algorithms, or complicated cycles of debt and loan repayment. Nor does it require you to move large sums of money from account to account or invest in refinancing schemes that end up creating more problems than they solve (Kagan, 2019).

The zero-based approach is exactly what it sounds like. It asks you to shut out all of the financial noise and simply start with a blank sheet of paper. For the zero-based approach, you only need to think about your business finances in two categories: income and expenses. All of the money that passes through company accounts is either money being earned or money being spent. What you do with that money ultimately depends on which category it belongs to.

Financial management doesn't need to be complicated, but it's often made unnecessarily complex. Too many companies try to take pre-existing models and apply them to their own finances, even though the financial realities facing your company may be very different from the realities facing another company (even if that company is part of the same industry). Especially in today's credit-based financial world, it's too tempting for companies to base their budgets on what they'll be earning in the future, rather than what they have in their accounts right now.

The zero-based model is a way for you to refocus your financial planning. Rather than looking at what you'll have next quarter, the zero-based model helps you to grow from what you have right now. Zero-based budgeting is about how to cover your expenses, grow your savings, and manage your investments with the money your business currently has. To many, this sounds impossible. How can you grow your business if you don't plan for the future, make investments, or take out loans? Believe it or not, not only is it possible, but it's actually the most secure way to grow your business. While other companies around you will fold under massive debt, unexpected costs, or become hamstrung by sudden changes in the market, your zero-based company will steadily weather any financial storm that comes its way.

Zero-based budgeting insists that all expenses must be justified for each new financial period. This might sound like a headache, but once you dive in, you'll be amazed at how many unnecessary expenses build up in a company budget over the course of a single financial period. A zero-based budget is also more tightly controlled. You will never find yourself losing money to automated payments that you didn't even realize your company was paying. You'll never lose money in obscure accounts that you forgot about or to sudden dips in investment accounts that you haven't been monitoring. The overwhelming and ever-changing landscape of your finances will become crystal clear.

Zero-based budgeting brings you back to... well, back to zero. The zero-based plan takes the overwhelming monster of your company's accounts and makes financial planning simple, logical, and realistic. Zero-based budgeting focuses you on what you are making and helps you to budget your money based on your real-time earnings. It eliminates any financial planning based on what you could be, should be, or will be making. Again, this goes against much conventional business-finance advice. At first, the zero-based method will seem totally strange to you. It may feel like a step back or seem far too simple for your business goals. But over time, you'll begin to see your company grow exponentially, and you'll see it growing in real profits and capital. While other companies may be growing faster than yours, their growth is often based on credit and investments, both of which can easily fold with unexpected costs or sudden changes in the market. The zero-based model starts you at zero and builds up your company with a solid financial foundation that cannot be shaken by external changes.

Following a zero-based budget means analyzing every function within your company for its needs and its costs. By focusing on real-time expenditures and periodic budget evaluations, you will be able to determine with certainty whether a certain service, investment, department, or project is enhancing or inhibiting your business. Rather than letting something grow and grow until it's too late to change, you will be able to spot problems very early on. This, in turn, keeps your company safely growing in the right direction while minimizing the risks of trying new things.

Where once managing your finances may have seemed overwhelming, the zero-based plan will make it simple, logical, and practical. Even better, once you've mastered the zero-based approach to finances, you can take this simple principle and apply it across your business. From organization to design, the zero-based approach can help to smooth out any area of business management, no matter how complicated or out-of-control it may feel right now.

While the zero-based principle is a surprisingly old model, it's quickly coming back into fashion now with the rise of digital technology. Thanks to computers, implementing the zero-based principle is easier than it's ever been. Coupling digital transformation with a zero-based model generates a virtuous cycle of earning that will help your company grow much faster than you ever believed possible.

However, the zero-based model isn't foolproof. Some companies have tried to implement it and still ended up with out-of-control finances. While it's a simple model, it does take a bit of guidance to master. This book will walk you through some of the common mistakes companies make when implementing the zero-based plan. It will also help you to tailor the zero-based model to meet your company's unique needs, not only in finances, but across the management spectrum.

No matter how big or small your company, a zero-based plan can work for you. With a little patience, this plan can transform your company into a zero-based workplace. Whether you are a first-time financial planner, a CFO in a huge corporation, or a small business owner feeling the inevitable strain of a rapidly growing business, you've come to the right place. The zero-based principle will help you to get back on track and back in control of your profits, loans, investments, savings, and expenditures.

CHAPTER1: WHAT IS ZERO-BASED BUDGETING?

Zero-based budgeting is a broad-reaching cost transformation effort. It affects all parts of your financial effort and is a planning system that tracks every penny, account, loan, and investment your business has. Zero-based budgeting is sometimes referred to as a "blank sheet of paper" approach, and that may be the most accurate way to look at it. In a zero-budget plan, you begin your plan completely from zero. In the simplest terms, you look at your company's net monthly income (so after taxes, how much money exactly does your company pull in?). Then, you list your company's expenses, beginning with the most essential. This stage is critical. Most essential means most essential. If you don't make X payment, your company will go out of business. Essential expenses are things like rent, utilities, and employee wages, and then things like loan payments. If your essential expenses equal or exceed your monthly income, all other expenses must be cut, suspended, or eliminated entirely. If you still have more money to spend after the essential expenses are covered, then you can make decisions as to how to spend the remaining money, whether that means saving, investing, or funding a new project. The process of actually creating a zero-based budget will be provided in more detail later in this book, but this is the barebones idea.

What makes zero-based budgeting so radically different from a traditional budget, however, is that a zero-based budget requires you to recreate this same ground-up model for every single financial period. That's right. Every year (or even every quarter, but that's not strictly necessary), you will rebuild your company budget from scratch, using the same "blank sheet of paper" mentality (Cruze, 2019). This bottom-up approach might sound like it's a lot of work, but it's this regular re-evaluation of company expenses that makes zero-based planning so successful. Every year, the budget is completely recalibrated to account for how much money the company actually has at that moment, rather than making small adjustments in obvious places. The traditional model of financial planning asks the accountant to run on a sort of auto-pilot. The mentality is to only adjust the budget if it's necessary. In a traditional financial model, increases or decreases in spending are adjusted in small increments over a preexisting budget. But in today's rapidly changing world, the revenue streams of last year could be completely different the following year. Investments that were profitable 10 years ago may suddenly plunge in value. The company that has no way to cope with these sudden changes will go under, while the company that carefully rebuilds its budget every year won't even blink at these radical changes – it will just make the necessary adjustments the way that it always does.

The approach of yearly rebuilding the budget isn't always easy, especially in the beginning. Agreements have to be made on the nature of costs, the appropriate places for reinvestment, and maintaining transparency on actual expenditures. A successful zero-based budget also requires a model of dual ownership over costs. Category owners and budget owners must have equal responsibility and decision-making power over expenditures, and complete transparency must be maintained at all times. If something is going to cost more or less than expected, then that reality cannot be concealed for the sake of preserving the budget.

A ZBB (zero-based budget) program can initiate radical changes in a company's approach to money management. It challenges the status-quo by asking all costs to be evaluated and defended. Only the most essential costs receive funding without question – everything else must be agreed upon. As such, ZBB can be a powerful tool for initiating policy changes, renegotiating prices, and aligning targets. It brings with it a company unity. All those involved understand the company's financial situation clearly, and so understand what needs to be done in order for the company to grow. This, in turn, will launch quicker negotiating wins, promote larger company initiatives, and even assist in the implementation of more accurate tracking tools.

ZBB forces managers to carefully examine every single expenditure. All but the most essential items must be defended if they are to be kept in the budget from year to year. Every cost is measured against both previous results and current expectations. Those costs that are deemed non-value-adding are eliminated from the budget. This allows for a radical redesign of company cost structures that are based on the company's actual earnings. If there are certain expenses that everyone wants, but that currently exceed the budget, then everyone can work toward hitting a certain financial target in order to work the desired initiative into next year's budget. Therefore, ZBB also encourages competitiveness within companies, as all departments have a clear understanding of what their budget is and how much they need to make in order to preserve that budget into the following year.

ZBB promotes the yearly analysis of all business activities, and helps managers to make the best decisions as to which activities should be performed at what levels and frequency. It also asks managers to examine how these activities can be better performed, which in turn encourages streamlining, standardization, outsourcing, offshoring, automation, and other efficiency-boosting procedures. In the past, ZBB was often used by companies as a way to confront conventional models of resource allocation by challenging every single line item. In a ZBB model, nothing is taken for granted, and so nothing is allowed to slip under the radar and clog up what could be an efficient and focused business.

Today, ZBB is used across the business world as a tool for simplification and rationalization of businesses whose financial planning has become overly complex. Most often, a zero-based plan is implemented after a merger or acquisition, as the overnight growth can throw the tightest of budgets into unmanageable chaos. However, no matter where you are in the life of your company, ZBB can be utilized to ensure the funding of key strategic imperatives by removing large non-value-adding costs and aligning resource allocation with the mission of efficient functionality. In a zero-based model, costs that drain away valuable resources are eliminated, while new initiatives are proposed with the company's current financial standing in mind. This connects the company's budget with its top-level strategic goals. The entire company is structured around the achieving of its goals, and those goals are set based on realistic financial expectations.

Most importantly, zero-based budgeting ensures that growth or value-enhancing costs can be covered by the company's current earnings. This virtually eliminates the possibility of taking out loans that are impossible for the company to pay or (literally) banking on unstable investments. There is no room in a zero-based budget for loans that can't be paid with the company's current earnings. If an investment comes back with a smaller return than expected, the company budget is simply adjusted accordingly, and the worth of the investment is examined in a way that it wouldn't be in a traditional financial model. Though ZBB can seem prohibitive for businesses that are small or that have gotten themselves into a great deal of debt, the long-term benefits provide both growth and security that are based on internal revenue, rather than on external factors like market values, interest rates, or economic trends.

CHAPTER 2: THE ZERO-BASED APPROACH

The zero-based approach asks a company to look at its expenditures through two key lenses: effectiveness (What do we expect this cost to accomplish for the organization?) and efficiency (How will this cost promote a lean and responsive organization?). Any cost that drains more value than it adds is eliminated as unnecessary. By looking at expenditures in this way, companies can capture significant efficiencies while upgrading capabilities and increasing value across company functions. In other words, the highest-value roles within the organization are clearly identified. These roles can then be staffed with the most qualified workers in order to promote talent in the company's most profitable departments.

ZBB, therefore, is far more thorough than traditional performance improvement programs. The traditional approach is to make incremental improvements above a pre-existing budget. The problem with this is that it does not ask management to examine which costs from the previous year's budget added value to the company and which created a drain in resources. The traditional model also results in incremental increases in spending regardless of how much the company's income has increased (or decreased). Instead of adjusting expenses to be more in-line with company growth, traditional adjustments often result in unrealistic budget expectations and an organization swollen with hidden costs or value-draining initiatives (Callaghan, 2014).

The shift to ZBB often results in a new operating model that empowers employees and can enable the reallocation of as much as 40% of staff spending to other areas. Projects, initiatives, and other costs that don't prove themselves to be value-adding are eliminated quickly. The money that they drained out of the company can be reinvested into other parts of the company that do promote growth. Anything that leeches resources out of the company can be pruned away, while anything that improves the value of the company can continue to be promoted.

To implement ZBB effectively, your company will need to go through a simple five-step process to evaluate exactly how this new plan can be best incorporated into your organization. These five steps are the core of ZBB and will be used by your company every year to reevaluate expenditures and rebuild the company budget using fresh financial data. These five steps are as follows:

1. Re-envision
2. Build a fact base
3. The blank sheet of paper
4. Build a future state
5. Reset budgets

Re-envision

The first step in ZBB is to re-envision the business. Ask what activities and resources are truly essential for your company to compete under both current and projected market conditions. This, in turn, will help you to set a clear strategic vision for your company and an appropriate cost target to make that vision possible. This first step is key, as it asks you to reorient your company and evaluate where it sits in the wider scheme of the marketplace. It's this first step that makes zero-based budgeting so flexible and so stable at the same time. Sudden changes or unexpected economic shifts will be accounted for here in this first stage. The company vision will be appropriately adjusted to meet current market realities and current projected trends, rather than relying on financial models that were designed with market data from 10, 15, or even 20 years ago.

Build a fact base

A comprehensive fact base is an updated list of current offerings, functions, and expenses. This gives you a thorough and up-to-date understanding of your company's current flow of revenue. It tells you where the company's money is going, where it needs to go, and where it could go if certain offerings or initiatives are worked into the current budget. You can think of your fact base as a guiding map of your company's current economic state. The fact base gives you a clear understanding of where your company is at the current moment. This exercise is critical because so much of financial planning involves projections into the future. Managers and financial planners spend just as much time thinking about what the company will be making as they do thinking about what the company is making. The fact sheet brings the entire company back to reality. Before you can make feasible plans for growth, you have to first understand where the company is right now.

The blank sheet of paper

Step three is where the real budgeting work is done. It's at this point where the company rebuilds its budget from zero, or from the "blank sheet of paper." The company's current income is weighted against its current expenses. All costs are defended in terms of necessity to the company, and all costs are adjusted in order to allocate the most resources to the most value-adding activities. This helps you to build the "ideal state." It ensures that all of your company's current expenditures can be covered by its current revenue streams. It then helps you to prioritize vital initiatives that will push your company toward a clear financial target. If said target is hit, then your company budget will be much bigger the following year. If it's not, then you can rest assured that next year's evaluation will cut, adjust, or streamline any initiatives that didn't work as well as they could have. Taking this approach every single pay period means adjusting your company's budget according to its actual earnings. While the traditional method advocates a blanket increase or decrease in spending, the "blank sheet of paper" method increases spending in certain beneficial areas, while decreasing spending in areas that aren't beneficial or that don't need the funding to continue functioning.

Build a future state

The "future state" is the projected state of the company in the following year. In order to push the company toward its "future state" goals, all company activities have to be evaluated against their promotion of this "future state." Any activities that don't promote the company's strategic goals are cut, adjusted, or absorbed into other departments.

Reset budgets

This is the final stage of the ZBB approach. In this stage, you form action plans and make the necessary adjustments to implement the new budget into company policy. All budgets, including full-time employee levels, are finalized and adjusted with the company's strategic mission in mind.

After many years of following the zero-based plan, this detail-oriented approach to budgeting is a well-oiled machine. However, when it's first implemented, it can require some radical shifts in company thinking, policy, and mindset. Therefore, many companies that adopt ZBB choose to implement it as a rolling process drawn out over several years. Rather than changing the entire company structure all at once, many companies break the organization down into smaller functional areas, that are reviewed one at time by managers and/or group leaders on a rolling basis. Instead of rebuilding the entire company budget from the ground up every year, the budget of one piece of the company is rebuilt from the ground up every few years.

Whether you implement ZBB on a large or a small scale, it's undoubtedly more time-consuming than the traditional method of financial planning. However, what your company may lose in time it will make back tenfold in costs. Instead of issuing blanket increases or decreases based on a pre-existing budget, costs are carefully examined on a regular basis to ensure that all areas of the company are performing at peak efficiency.

CHAPTER 3: WHAT NOT TO DO: WHEN ZERO-BASED BUDGETING IS APPLIED INCORRECTLY

Zero-based budgeting isn't a foolproof system. There are some common mistakes that many businesses make when attempting to budget this way. The first (and most common) is using the zero-based model as a one-time fix. Many, many businesses use ZBB to successfully reassess their budgets, but then revert back to the traditional model of blanket increases or decreases in spending over the following years. In order for the zero-based method to work, it has to be done periodically. For many businesses, restructuring the budget of the entire company is wildly impractical. Many corporations don't even calculate their budgets in a company-wide scheme, choosing instead to break financial planning into smaller functional areas within the company. If you feel that the zero-based approach is too radical for your company, this is not a problem. Instead of applying the zero-based method to the entire company every single year, a feasible alternative is to break the company budget into smaller functional areas. Every financial period, only one functional area is brought back to zero with the "blank sheet of paper" method. Cycling through the functional areas each financial period will ensure that all areas of the company benefit from the zero-based approach. Individual departments may end up restructuring their budget every three or even five years, rather than every single year, but in big multinational corporations this is actually more efficient than trying to restructure the entire company budget on an annual basis.

Regardless of how you choose to cycle it, the zero-based method can only work if the budget is periodically restructured. There are a few reasons for this. It's definitely valuable to challenge, justify, and prioritize all company or department expenses. However, there are some expenses that may seem important, but ultimately turn out to be more draining than initially expected (Schwahn, 2019). If the budget is never revisited, these draining expenses will never be adjusted, and your company will end up right back where it started – with unmanageable finances and out-of-control expenditures. Applying ZBB in fixed periods also greatly minimizes the financial risks associated with new projects or initiatives. The only way to evaluate the success of a newly proposed activity or adjustment is to revisit it. If the budget is never brought back to zero, then evaluating the success of new projects becomes far more difficult. Too many companies end up pulling funding from value-adding projects because they can't fit the cost of the new project into the proposed spending increase. However, if the budget was built from the bottom up, with all expenses being individually examined and justified, then the worth of these value-adding projects would be recognized, and therefore, funding them would be appropriately prioritized.

The second biggest mistake that companies make when applying ZBB is cutting costs too aggressively. One of the basic principles of ZBB is that company expenses cannot outweigh company income. However, companies sometimes cut so many costs that employees begin to feel like the company is actually struggling financially. This, in turn, has a negative impact on employee morale. Negative employee morale can have devastating effects on company efficiency, which will negatively impact company profits, which will mean even more cuts when ZBB is applied the following year. In other words, aggressively cutting costs can send the company into a negative spiral that severely cripples the company's ability to grow or hit proposed financial targets.

To avoid this, it's important that all managers agree on which costs are absolutely essential for the company to function, and it's equally important that those costs continue to be funded. Putting money into savings, believe it or not, cannot be considered an essential cost. Contrary to conventional financial wisdom, the zero-budget method insists that if you have to spend your entire income in order to cover essential costs, then spend it. If your budget is truly funding value-adding functions, then your company or department will find itself with a bigger monthly income to work with the next time ZBB is applied. This, in turn, will mean that you will not only have all of your essential costs covered, but your company has sufficiently grown to the point that you can begin putting money into savings. Crippling company functionality in order to save will cause your company to shrink, not grow. If you have to go a few years without a savings, so be it. As long as you have a certain amount being put into an emergency fund, it's far better to fund value-adding functions than it is to cut value-adding functions in order to pad the company savings account.

The third biggest mistake that executives make when implementing ZBB is skipping the first and second steps and going straight to the "blank sheet of paper" stage. However, ZBB isn't just a budget – it's a mindset. Most of the work done in ZBB is actually changing the company mindset, rather than changing the company budget. In order for ZBB to work effectively, everyone involved must agree on financial targets and company goals. Otherwise, prioritizing which costs are more or less important will be impossible. When evaluating costs in the "blank sheet of paper" stage, these costs must be evaluated against the company goals. "How much does this cost promote the company vision?" is the primary question that must be asked when discussing every expenditure. If the company vision has not been clearly outlined, then making these kinds of evaluations will be impossible to do in an efficient way.

Those who view ZBB as a simple financial tool, rather than a radical transformation of the company's cost management approach, are prone to making the first two mistakes. Ignoring the mindset adjustments crucial to ZBB often result in companies doing an excellent job of restructuring their finances during the initial application, and then reverting back to old spending patterns in the following financial periods. Using ZBB as a simple financial model and ignoring the goal-setting stages also makes companies far more likely to cut costs too severely. Clinging too tightly to the numbers, without having a clear direction as to what purpose those numbers server, will inevitably result in bad decisions. Functions, activities, and even people who are incredibly value-adding can be cut in a zero-based budget that doesn't have a clear understanding of the company's goals.

Applying ZBB without agreement on what the company's goals are is like going on a crash diet and then going right back to unhealthy lifestyle habits once the desired weight loss target is reached. In order for ZBB to bring long-term financial security and growth to your company, it must be applied periodically, and always in the context of company goals. ZBB is not just a budget change, it's a company culture change. It's not only the company budget that needs to be rebuilt from the bottom up but the company mindset. If everyone in the company doesn't have a clear understanding of the company's goals, then it won't matter how strictly the company adheres to the proposed numbers. Cutting costs will only work if everyone agrees that those expenditures are not as important as the functions being prioritized.

CHAPTER 4: TIPS FOR SUCCESS: HOW TO OPTIMIZE THE ZERO-BASED APPROACH FOR YOUR ORGANIZATION

Once a company commits to the zero-based method, the obvious approach is to solve immediately pressing problems. It's often much easier to reach an agreement on what the company's problems are than on what the company's goals should be. As a result, many of the initial benefits of ZBB are technical – creating new links between previously isolated financial-data systems, for example, or integrating thousands of spreadsheets into a single budgeting platform. These kinds of problems are crucial to solve, and there's no doubt that this is one of the biggest benefits of ZBB implementation. However, solving these kinds of problems isn't enough. To fully implement ZBB, it's not just technical problems that need to be solved. The entire company culture must be changed. If everyone is not given enough time or information to reorient themselves to the new vision, then they will inevitably revert back to their problematic spending habits.

The most important component of ZBB success is implementing zero-based culture, not just zero-based methodology. Being 100% transparent about budgets, spending, and finances is completely alien to most people. As such, almost every business is going to need time to practice new behaviors and objectively evaluate the results of the new system. Many executives, managers, and financial planners are used to routinely hiding funds in budget lines that they know won't ever be closely examined. This doesn't make them lazy or incompetent workers. Rather, the traditional blanket-statement method of financing almost encourages this kind of behavior. In the traditional model, once the spending increase is decided upon, it's up to leaders to make sure that money is made. If the proposed percentage is made, then the methods used to achieve that increase are never scrutinized (Blakely-Gray, 2017).

In the zero-based methodology, on the other hand, complete transparency is absolutely critical to success. If something is going to cost more than expected, that needs to be honestly communicated. In the traditional model, people are typically disciplined for failing to meet the expected financial targets. This discipline-based approach encourages dishonesty and fosters a corporate culture of deception. However, in the zero-based method, transparency is encouraged. Honesty and communication are valued above all. If something is not working, it's best to catch it early, so that it can be cut or modified in order to keep it in line with the overall company vision.

Revealing these habits of cost hiding and financial deception is frightening at first. Implementing ZBB means committing to aggressive cost and value targets, both of which can do a great deal to disrupt the established methods of management in a company. Success can only be achieved, however, when the zero-based budget is integrated into workplace methodology. Everyone should be asking themselves the same question: "What can I do to achieve the company's goals?"

It's only when this mindset is achieved that the zero-based method stops feeling radical, uncomfortable, or disruptive. Once everyone is on the same page, then a once disparate and disorganized company will begin to run in a seamless, well-oiled fashion. When everyone in the company understands what the targets are and is doing their best to achieve those targets, that's when companies begin to grow at exponential rates. That target may move slightly from year to year, but morale, efficiency, and profits are always at their highest when the entire company understands what is most important for success.

In order for the zero-based method to succeed in your business, it has to become routine. There will always be an adjustment period. But once your company makes the transition from a traditional routine to a zero-based routine, you will begin to see your company grow and thrive at rates you never thought possible. To make the zero-based method a zero-based culture, this methodology has to be demonstrated from the top levels all the way down to the company's smallest employee. It has to be communicated consistently and clearly and reinforced with genuine accountability. Sometimes it's necessary to discipline employees for behaving in a way that runs contrary to the company mission. However, the moment someone is disciplined for transparency, trust in the system will collapse, and you will find yourself in the position of rebuilding a zero-based culture from scratch.

Support for new capabilities, initiatives, and programs is also a key component of the zero-based approach. With the security that regular evaluates provides must also come a willingness to experiment. Allowing people to prove that their proposed projects will add value to the company gives them a level of autonomy they would never have under a traditional financial model. In a zero-based culture, everyone has input as to how the finances may be best used. Therefore, everyone needs a chance to prove that their suggestions can be backed by real company profits and growth. If their suggestions are not found to be value-adding the next time the budget is evaluated, then the company has only learned from its experimentation and has a better understanding of which activities are sustainable and which are not.

Jim Collins advises all business people to invest (always) in people before capital (Correa, 2015). Young and talented leaders can make or break a company, but if the company culture prohibits those with real talents from shining, then it will continue to suffer from weak leadership and bad decision making. Using ZBB to promote talent within your company is one of the most efficient ways to use this tool to transform your company's budget and culture. Routinely evaluating and examining all company expenditures makes it clear which parts of the company are value-adding and which are not. This, in turn, can help you to focus on staffing the value-adding parts of the company with talented people, ensuring that those areas continue to grow and contribute to the company's success.

ZBB can also be used to give young leaders the ability to try new projects or initiatives. In a zero-based company, everyone knows that they will eventually have to justify the costs of their activities. This encourages all employees to plan and propose new ideas more carefully, which increases their chance of success. It also means that, if a project or initiative fails, the financial loss incurred is minimal. Because of the radical transparency inherent in a zero-based workplace, everyone will understand exactly what caused that project to fail. Everyone involved will have a better understanding of what steps need to be taken to ensure success in future endeavors. This means that, even if the company loses money, it still grows in terms of business or management wisdom. Companies that don't take risks eventually become trapped in old ways of thinking. But if you use ZBB to fund new projects and invest in new leaders, your company will always be adapting and learning from its mistakes.

The zero-based method is most successful when it is used to evaluate both expenditures and attitudes. Setting goals, and prioritizing expenses in the service of that goal, sustains company momentum. It promotes the retention of ambitious people because it gives them big goals to strive for, and it facilitates company growth because it focuses the entire business, no matter how big or small, on a particular achievement. In traditional companies, budget cuts and spending decreases often have a negative impact on company morale. But if you apply ZBB to both finances and attitudes, then budget cuts will actually improve your company's morale. Budget cuts will feel like progress, not regression. People will be glad to see the company removing things that don't add value so that everyone can focus on the bigger goal. Those who can't cooperate to achieve the agreed targets will eventually leave your company, while those who are focused, cooperative, and hardworking will remain with you for a long time.

CHAPTER 5: THE BENEFITS OF ZERO-BASED BUDGETING

The zero-based approach doesn't just change your company's cost management system. It also challenges the way the company chooses decision-making rights, targets, and incentives. When ZBB is successfully integrated into the company culture, it becomes the spine of the company's entire business strategy. ZBB aligns the company's budget with both its current realities and its goals, something that other budgeting models fail to do. Achieving this alignment can take some time, but once the company fully transitions to a zero-based culture, it will begin to reap some very real benefits.

Sustainable Growth and Value Creation

Sustainable growth comes from money saved being reinvested back into the business's value drivers. This creates a virtuous cycle that simultaneously improves bottom-line and top-line performance. Every time the zero-based method is applied, spending is shifted from wasteful or low-impact areas to places where it will generate top-line growth. This growth means a bigger budget to work with in the following financial period, which then means the business has even more money to invest back into its value drivers.

Applied correctly, ZBB facilitates the reinvestment of company money into activities that drive new sales and add value to the company. In ZBB, differentiated costs go far beyond reducing headcount or slashing departmental budgets. Instead, companies focus on cuts that will both have a positive impact on company performance and cause little or no collateral damage. So, for example, if reducing headcount means losing valuable people or dramatically increasing the workload of the remaining employees, then reducing headcount is not a cut that will leave a positive impact on the company. In a ZBB company, another solution would be found to reduce unnecessary spending while retaining valuable members of the company.

New Operating Models

In the zero-based approach, companies set financial benchmarks by taking a bottom-up view of priorities and opportunities. This facilitates cross-functional communication and often results in a change of the entire operating model. Instead of making isolated modifications to a particular line item, the entire budget is viewed as an interconnected system. Spending in one particular area has implications for the entire company. Traditional models are often blind to these connections until it's too late. In the ZBB approach, however, new operating models are created with ease and implemented with efficiency.

A huge benefit of ZBB is the focus on simplifying processes so that the most time and effort can be spent on activities that add real value to the business. For example, bonus structures are often complex and require a great deal of subjective oversight from managers. If the company is committed to retaining and rewarding talented people, however, a complex system based on subjective observations can leave many people feeling frustrated or undervalued. Streamlining the bonus process to rely on a few discrete metrics achieves several goals at once. First, it puts the achievement of bonus pay within the control of the individual employee. Each worker will know exactly what needs to be done to earn that extra pay. This frees up managers and leaders to spend their time and effort in other areas. Finally, it makes bonus pay much easier to budget for as it will be clear to all what exactly needs to be done to earn that pay. This will make it far easier to predict how much bonus pay the company can reasonably expect to issue at the end of the pay period.

In a traditional budgeting model, the bonus process is often set from the beginning and is never re-evaluated. This means that employees are rewarded, not for the work they do, but based on how much extra money the company decides it has at the end of the year. Those who work hard may get no recognition in lean years, while those who don't add value may reap huge bonuses simply for being in high-level positions. This model breeds distrust between employees and managers, and between middle-management and executives. It also means that large sums of money tend to be invested in people who aren't necessarily adding value to the company, which means that the company will end up retaining inefficient workers and losing talented leaders. ZBB, on the other hand, asks the company to examine every single expense and that includes bonuses. In this example, the bonus structure was reworked to bring it more closely in line with company values, to make it more financially feasible given the company's current earnings, and to increase financial transparency throughout the company.

This is just one example of how the ZBB mindset can streamline and optimize your company for the better. Making continuous changes might sound like chaos, and it is if those changes aren't made in the service of specific goals. However, when ZBB changes are applied, they are always done in the service of aligning spending with company goals and values. This creates a company culture that embraces adaptations, beneficial adjustments, and new ways of thinking.

Better Customer-Company Relationships

The changes that are made in a zero-based budget don't only affect internal operations - they affect the company's relationship with the customer as well. Funding value-adding activities often directly translates to improvements in company services, product value, and customer satisfaction. It's not only employees that are made aware of the company's goals – the customers also begin to have a better awareness of what your business is about and what kinds of services it wants to offer in the future. Companies that are seen to be growing, innovating, and improving attract the most business, while companies that seem stagnant or unchanging often struggle to attract new buyers.

For example, perhaps your company agrees to change the terms of customer credit. The approved change is to reduce variations with the goals of minimizing the need for manual interventions and reducing the risk of human error. These changes benefit your company in a number of ways. The time and effort spent on interventions and damage control can now be spent in other ways. The inevitable costs associated with risk management are now greatly reduced. And the terms are simpler, making them easier for sales consultants to remember, explain, and sell.

However, these changes also benefit your customers. A more streamlined credit offering is much easier for customers to understand. This new simplicity makes it easier for customers to evaluate whether they want to open a credit line with your business. It also makes them more confident when asking questions or meeting with sales consultants. This also enables you to gain more honest feedback from customers that you can then use to improve your services even more. It increases customer trust in your company, which makes them far more willing to do business with you. It also makes them more willing to recommend your business to others, providing you with new customers without a cent being spent on advertising.

In a traditional model, these large-scale modifications are difficult to propose and even more difficult to implement. The kind of thorough evaluation that ZBB encourages brings these problems into the light. When all expenses are weighed with equal consideration, opportunities to streamline emerge. Most importantly, when everyone has a clear understanding of what kind of relationship the company wants to have with its customers, then large-scale shifts can be made quickly and efficiently. In a ZBB company, everyone is on the same page. Everyone understands what needs to be changed and why. This understanding will make your company extraordinarily adaptable. The ability to make quick changes or adjustments with little upset gives your company a competitive edge that is difficult for more rigidly-structured companies to keep up with.

CHAPTER 6: ZERO-BASED 2019 – HOW TO AUGMENT THE ZERO-BASED APPROACH WITH DIGITAL TECHNOLOGY

D igital transformation is the process of using technology and automation to streamline company processes. Many contemporary companies are finding that automation fits neatly into a zero-based plan. First, automation can help companies to save costs in a number of different departments. When operating models are revamped, each company activity is analyzed to determine at what levels and frequencies these activities should be performed. Technology and digitization can then be incorporated into these activities in order to facilitate efficient ROI (Return on Investment).

In the contemporary business world, using digital technology to streamline company processes is called digital transformation, and it's hardly uncommon. As far back as 2013, companies like BNP Paribas, HSBC, and AXA each invested more than $3 million dollars into digital transformation. No one is surprised when technology is used to simplify business processes or reduce system complexities. In fact, it's more uncommon for a company *not* to be investing huge chunks of its budget into digital transformation programming, in CAPEX or OPEX.

However, many companies are pushing the bounds of digital technology, finding more and more ways that technology can be introduced into company processes to increase business efficiency. Many of these companies are zero-based companies, open to and eager for more advanced technologies that can further streamline company processes. Cognitive systems are programs that perform more complex tasks beyond the capabilities of a simple computer. Often these systems are augmented with AI (artificial intelligence) technology that actually help the program to make decisions. This technology may sound futuristic, but AI has successfully been used by companies around the world to review resumes and even interact with customers via email or even over the phone. Decision management programs are AIs that can (given the proper input) make low-level management decisions and propose adjustments to company rules, policies, or parameters. AIs can even be used in supply chain models to enable on-demand fulfillment, and subsequently free up working capital cash.

Funding these advanced technologies can be a difficult balance. Spending significant sums of money on digital technology can deteriorate margins or divert funding from acquisitions and new market opportunities. To combat this, management often requests savings at a pace concurrent with the necessary investments in digital technology.

This is where the zero-based company has the advantage. Starting from the "blank sheet of paper" means challenging all costs, both direct and indirect. Prioritizing all company initiatives and activities means understanding which activities could benefit the most from digitization and which activities can be cut without a negative impact on the company. As such, the zero-based company can fund digital transformation programs by cutting unnecessary costs, rather than trying to spread funding across multiple areas or diverting funding from value-adding activities like acquisitions. More importantly, the zero-based company can also feel confident that the money invested in digital transformation is well spent, as the ZBB process ensures that the most funding goes to the most important activities.

However, digital transformation isn't always about adding new technologies. Sometimes updating old methods is required as well. Many, many traditional companies get bogged down in outdated technology or fail to successfully integrate new technological solutions. The ZBB culture of examining and justifying every cost, however, often reveals new opportunities to update and improve existing technologies. A good example of this is software updates. Most traditional budgets include a line for the renewal of software licenses. However, licensure costs are often increased by the provider every pay period. These increasing costs are either accepted without question by the traditional model, or (worse) are hidden under the "blanket increase" model of spending.

ZBB companies, on the other hand, have to examine every cost, including the cost of software licensure. Zero-based budgeters are far more likely to realize that the cost of licensure is steadily increasing and are therefore encouraged to look for other software options or to negotiate other delivery options with the current provider. This opens up opportunities to introduce new software that will streamline overall company performance and/or negotiate new licensure agreements that create savings.

Whether it's updating current technologies or seeking out entirely new ones, ZBB is often an initiator of digital transformation. Increasingly, zero-based companies are more and more willing to pioneer new technologies and successfully incorporate them into their business model. First, ZBB companies have the flexibility and open-mindset required to experiment with cutting-edge technology in the workplace. Second, ZBB companies are highly focused on how to optimize their company to achieve the best results with the lowest costs. Therefore, these companies often best understand how to use this technology to improve business efficiency, and are committed to implementing this technology without damaging the workplace culture or replacing valuable employees with digital programs. And finally, the zero-based model encourages companies to continuously evaluate how much the technology is actually contributing to the business. Because of this, zero-based companies rarely get stuck investing in technological systems that are complex, glitchy, or prone to error. Simultaneously, ZBB companies are more likely to end up with high-quality technology that does indeed improve the quality of work, drive sales, and actively contribute to company growth.

In short, ZBB helps to fund digitization programs or investments by generating savings on recurring activities and often initiating the transformation in the first place. However, for this to be most successful, the ZBB process itself must be augmented with digital technology. Digitizing the ZBB process streamlines the process across the board, and (perhaps ironically) makes room for better streamlining technologies in the future.

When following the ZBB process, when deciding which activities to digitize, the team should ask three essential questions: "How does this activity contribute to the company?," "Can this activity be digitized?," and "How is it possible to automate or streamline this process with digital technology?" This will help your company to identify digital levers of performance and build your zero-based budget at the same time.

Working digital transformation into your ZBB will also serve to empower managers by encouraging them to clearly define their digital initiatives and objectives. Successfully incorporating digital transformation into a zero-based plan requires identifying which activities will have the best returns on investment, and so strengthens the ZBB methods of identifying company values and changing corporate culture. Zero-based budgets naturally encourage companies to cut out unnecessary managerial layers and develop a customer-centric mindset. Digital transformation is a natural facilitator of these kinds of initiatives, and so ZBB companies that incorporate digital transformation programs seem to benefit exponentially from the streamlining opportunities that digitalization provides.

However, the ZBB process itself can be complex and cumbersome. It often takes several months to complete the process successfully, and it's something that must be done periodically in order to achieve optimum results. Because of the money and time needed for ZBB, many companies have decided not to do it annually, and instead install it every three or even five years. Digitizing ZBB itself, then, becomes a natural solution to the budgeting problem. With the help of digital programming, the ZBB process itself can be performed much faster and with less resource consumption. This, in turn, makes it possible to build a ZBB more frequently, optimizing its benefits and contributing to company growth. Setting a new Target Operating Model for a Digital Finance is often the best way to do this. This will speed up the overall process by reviewing cost and investment projections in a more integrated way.

CHAPTER 7: BEYOND BUDGETING – APPLYING THE ZERO-BASED METHOD TO OTHER MANAGEMENT TOOLS

The zero-based budget is successful because it's not only about cost management – when most successful, it changes the entire company mindset. In recent years, the psychology behind zero-based budgeting has been expanded and applied to other management areas. Introducing the zero-based mindset into other levels of management can be an extremely effective way to focus the company on its goals and lesson the shock of implementing the zero-based budget. Many companies even choose to implement the zero-based mindset into other areas first before implementing the zero-based budget.

Zero-Based Organization

While zero-based budgeting is about efficient reallocation of funding, zero-based organization (or ZBO) is about the efficient reallocation of more general resources. The zero-based budget helps to identify which areas are value-adding, and subsequently funnel money into those areas. However, sometimes the company structure can inhibit even the most efficiently budgeted organization. Siloed functions, redundant capabilities across business units, and mission creep are all organization defects that can impede profitability.

Much like zero-based budgeting, ZBO asks managers to rebuild their company structure from the bottom up. Rather than making adjustments to the preexisting structure, managers start from zero, organizing the company in a way that best facilitates company profits, culture, and growth. Unlike ZBB, ZBO does not have to be repeated periodically in order to be successful. To implement ZBO, managers must follow four basic steps:

1. Establish visibility
2. Ensure comprehensive benchmarking
3. Create strategy/capability links
4. The art of the possible

Establish visibility

Too often, business-unit leaders function in isolation. They are aware of their own department's growth, needs, and goals, but know shockingly little about what's happening in other departments. The number one step in implementing ZBO is to establish cross-departmental visibility. Resources should be viewed company wide, rather than being sectioned off into isolated departmental budgets. Determining staffing levels and assessing role definitions should be done with full transparency, and with consideration to the needs of the company as a whole, rather than focusing solely on the needs of the department. Establishing governance processes can help companies to monitor staffing variances over time, and so get a more accurate idea of where staffing is most needed.

Ensure comprehensive benchmarking

ZBO means rebuilding the structure from the bottom up. Goals, benchmarks, and evaluations must be done in a comprehensive way, giving thought to all aspects of the company structure. Organization size, pay grades, spans and layers, automation, interlinked activities, and function-specific productivity factors should all be taken into consideration. Using both internal and external data enables the most intelligent target setting by comparing productivity levels across units against two measurements: efficiency and effectiveness.

Create strategy/capability links

The ultimate goal of ZBO is to successfully pair organizational designs with strategic priorities. Rather than adjusting preexisting organizational models to fit new company visions, ZBO asks companies to build new organizational models that best facilitate the achievement of company goals. The reason that ZBO only has to be implemented once is because it asks managers to build organizational models that not only evaluate existing talent but reflect the talent that will be needed in the future. This makes the ZBO design far more flexible than traditional organization methods. ZBO structures can be easily merged, adjusted, or evaluated as needed, because they are built around the company's core principles and are implemented with both current and projected future realities in mind.

The art of the possible

ZBO can seem like a huge undertaking at first, but its initiation can act as a catalyst for radical new approaches to business organization. The implementation of ZBO fosters a company culture of innovation, encouraging managers to think beyond traditional models of organization. Inevitably, the result is a more agile and responsive organization that has a clear understanding of its current targets and can easily make large-scale adjustments to achieve new ones.

Zero-Based Design

Like ZBO, zero-based design (or ZBD) asks you to take a look at the way your company is structured. However, while ZBO is about rebuilding a preexisting company from the bottom up, ZBD is for those who are just starting out. Zero-based design asks start-ups, new business owners, and those still trying to get their ideas off the ground to apply the zero-based mindset to the initial design of their business.

This might seem a bit counter intuitive. After all, doesn't every new business venture start from zero? Technically yes, but too many new businesses are just iterations of traditional models. ZBD asks entrepreneurs to design every aspect of their business with their ultimate goals in mind. Rather than adjusting traditional models to fit your new business, ZBD insists on the complete marriage of design with strategy. All aspects of the business should be designed from the very beginning to best facilitate the goals of your new company. This established a zero-based culture right off the bat. New businesses are always extremely fragile when they enter the market, but ZBD companies tend to survive because they're inherently more flexible. ZBD companies are built with future targets in mind, so they can quickly make adjustments to survive the unexpected realities of the market.

Zero-Based Productivity

Zero-based productivity (or ZBP) extends the principles of ZBB to look, not only at spending, but at performance. ZBP (especially when paired with ZBB) can jump-start growth, improve financial performance, and empower managers with spending authority to continuously evaluate the quality of the work they oversee.

ZBP differs from traditional methods of productivity boosting in a few essential ways. First, it greatly improves visibility. ZBP asks for full transparency about performance across departments. Like ZBB, if you want to implement ZBP successfully, you should begin by creating a strong fact base. This will give you a good idea of not only what your company finances look like right now, but what your company's productivity looks like right now. Which cost categories are operating at the highest levels? Where is productivity stagnant, or even decreasing? Too many productivity-boosting or monitoring strategies are based on where the company *wants* productivity to increase, rather than where productivity *needs* to increase. This often results in a destruction of company morale, as value-adding departments being to feel pressured or over-worked, while low-productivity departments can feel neglected or develop toxic workplace mindsets.

Establishing this strong fact base then facilitates more intelligent target setting. While ZBB asks managers to reconsider spending, ZBP asks managers to reconsider constraints, policies, and decision-making power. Low-productivity areas are evaluated against their current targets. The traditional approach to productivity-boosting is "Why is this area not meeting its targets?" The zero-based approach, however, asks "How can this area best contribute to company growth?" Often, low-productivity areas are not producing good results because their targets are unrealistic or unachievable given the area's current reality. ZBP typically results in setting more sensible targets that reintegrate low-productivity areas into the greater company vision, transforming them into value-adding areas or merging them with other departments to form new value-adding structures.

Zero-Based Culture

Adopting a zero-based culture (or ZBC) means implementing the zero-based mindset across leadership tools. In a zero-based workplace culture, ZBB and ZBP are both used together to boost sales, reduce waste, and accelerate improvement. Leaders who adopt ZBC understand that zero-basing is not only about transparency and goal-oriented processes. It's also about governance, mindsets, and incentives that reinforce zero-based behavior and keep the entire company functioning as a cohesive unit.

Chapter 8: The Zero-Based Principle

The zero-based principle (sometimes called the zero-based approach) takes the ideas inherent in zero-based budgeting and extrapolates them across a company culture. The zero-based principle follows to basic ideas: there are no wasted parts of an organization and less is more.

There Are No Wasted Parts of an Organization

Every expenditure, every employee, every policy, every target, every sale, every customer... no matter what it is, all pieces of the company either contribute to or inhibit growth. Applying the zero-based principle is a quest to achieve complete cohesion within a company, where all people, functions, and expenses contribute to the fulfillment of company goals.

The zero-based principle maintains that long-term planning can only be successful in a culture of flexibility, dynamism, and adaptation. When applied successfully, the zero-based approach encourages leaders to shed their assumptions and think far outside the box. When adopted as a culture, the zero-based principle facilitates huge innovations in performance, cost management, and organizational design. Zero-basing is founded on the idea that all elements of the company must be working together toward the same goal. When this principle is not embraced, zero-basing can result in more red tape, more complexity, and lower investment.

The zero-based principle is fundamentally different from traditional management styles because it encourages transparency, autonomy, and flexibility. Traditional methods of business are strictly hierarchical. Those you directly report to should be told only what they want to hear, and those who directly report to you must be monitored for laziness, incompetence, or inefficiency at all times. However, the zero-based principle insists on complete transparency. All discussions must be fact-driven and based in current realities. Projections into the future must still be rooted in realities, and evaluated against company goals, rather than against departmental or even individual goals. As such, zero-based companies are often structured in more egalitarian, cooperative, and dynamic ways that enable the company to quickly promote and retain talent. Employees of zero-based companies often do far more work, yet simultaneously feel more valued, energized, and ambitious, than workers in more traditional companies.

As such, the zero-based principle fosters a workplace culture that generates success. When all aspects of the company are seen to be functioning in efficient cohesion, all employees are encouraged to make intelligent decisions, produce higher-quality work, and have much better relationships with customers or clients. From a financial perspective, the zero-based principle stops seeing expenditures in a black-and-white frame of "company success = increased spending" and "company challenges = decreased spending." In fact, zero-based companies often welcome cost cuts, structural changes, or digital transformation as exciting and beneficial! Traditional companies that try to implement similar changes, on the other hand, are often plagued by rigidity, uncertainty, and criticism.

The zero-based principle looks at all features of the company as important. This means that non-value-adding costs may be cut from the budget, but it also means that value-adding costs are prioritized. If every employee's contribution to the company is evaluated, then problems will be seen more quickly, but so too will talent. The zero-based principle enables mangers to have complete clarity, and to view their company as it is, not what it could or should be. Traditional companies tend to only implement change in order to solve problems. But zero-based companies are able to implement changes that facilitate growth. Dividing the company into the categories of value-adding and non-value-adding is not about dividing the company into "good" and "bad," "positive" or "negative." Instead, it's about the achievement of cohesion. Non-value-adding activities or functions are evaluated against what is best for the company. Should they be cut, merged, or streamlined? Would they become value-adding if they were digitized, automated, giving different targets, or restructured? The mindset of periodic evaluation is a mindset of growth and innovation. Flexibility is key in today's dynamic market. Companies with growth mindsets will continue to shift and adapt to the changing world, while companies with rigid mindsets will slowly find themselves unable to keep up.

Less Is More

Zero-based companies understand that a lot can be done with very little. Additional layers of complexity clog up company processes, slow down communications, and increase risk of error. Too many people on one project or activity can lower productivity. Too many departments can cripple decision-making and create communication gridlocks when department heads can't come to an agreement. And (of course) reducing expenditures ultimately leads to more savings.

Zero-basing can be a complicated process, especially in the beginning. However, this is often because it requires a massive shift in corporate culture and company thinking. Once the cultural shift has been made, the actual process of zero-basing moves much faster, especially if parts of the process are digitized. The underlying principle of the "blank sheet of paper" is to simplify and clarify corporate understanding of the company's finances. The "blank sheet of paper" asks financial managers to build their budget based on what is actually in front of them, a far easier task that building their budget based on what could or should be in front of them. Future predictions and targets also become much easier to set because they are based in reality and partnered with the company's overall goals. Instead of trying to manage a host of smaller departmental budgets or a financial plan based on hundreds of individual targets, the zero-based plan evaluates all company proceedings based on how they do (or don't) contribute to growth.

The goal with zero-based budgeting (and behind the zero-based principle in general) is not just to reduce indirect cost. Zero-basing means bringing the entire company back to zero, from revenue to profit margins to cash on hand. When the company is brought back to zero, it quickly becomes clear that there are many pieces of the company that aren't necessary. Shedding extraneous expenses often translates into shedding extraneous processes, steps, and functions. It encourages managers to evaluate how things can be done in faster and simpler ways. The simpler the model, the more efficient the process. Zero-basing prevents expenditures or functions from becoming hidden in the company model. Unnecessary costs, outdated technologies, and swollen departments can't survive a zero-based evaluation. The zero-based principle isn't just about saving money – it's about reinvesting money in more profitable ways.

The zero-based principle tends to favor areas that achieve direct revenues or production, as these areas are more easily justifiable. These areas are also much easier to streamline, benefit the most from digital transformation, and can often be achieved with fewer managerial layers. Departments like client services or research and development, on the other hand, can be much harder to justify in a zero-based evaluation. While these departments are sometimes erroneously cut altogether, the zero-based approach asks managers to be far more proactively involved in finding solutions and developing innovations than traditional business philosophies. As such, an R&D department may ultimately become unnecessary in a zero-based company because everyone in the company is focused on ways to develop and improve. Instead of relegating innovation to one department, the entire company becomes actively engaged in the implementation of improvements and new initiatives. The same can be said for client services. As the entire company adopts a growth mindset, relationships with clients and customers naturally improve. Rather than relegating customer service to one department, all members of the company become actively invested in promoting a positive customer experience.

CONCLUSION

Zero-based budgeting is a radical system of resource allocation that seeks to pair company spending with top-level goal setting. As such, ZBB goes far beyond a simple tool for cost management. Zero-basing is an entire mentality, that can be successfully used to change workplace culture to be more productive, agile, and innovative. There are four core main features of zero-basing, all of which are successfully implemented into a zero-based company to form a ZBC, or zero-based culture.

Redefining

Zero-based companies redefine spending based on evolving company needs and prioritize them against company values. To successfully implement a zero-based budget into your organization, the most important step is for you to clearly define your vision for the company as a whole. Without a clear understanding of the company mission, costs cannot be intelligently prioritized, and the zero-based process of simplification can end up creating more problems than it solves.

Challenging

Zero-based companies challenge all expenditures, following the philosophy that every line item has implications for company success. When implementing a zero-based budget, evaluate every cost from two perspectives: functional and operational.

Costs that are beneficial from both perspectives should be prioritized. Costs that are deemed to be non-value adding are typically cut altogether. However, sometimes solutions can be found through streamlining, merging, or automation. A digital transformation program can be a powerful tool when paired with ZBB. Digitization can streamline entire functional areas of companies and has implications for the productivity of an entire organization.

Creating

ZBB is about embracing change and welcoming creative solutions to problems. Fostering transparency, embracing digital technologies, and promoting new talent are all parts of a zero-based culture. Whether you are applying the zero-based principle to your budget, organization, design, or simply to your company culture at large, fostering a culture of flexibility is key to its success. Where traditional models often crumble when faced with unexpected market shifts or large-scale economic changes, zero-based companies are able to quickly adjust to evolving expectations.

Changing

Above all, zero-basing is a mindset. Changing mindsets by fostering radical accountability, transparency, and cross-departmental communications is critical to the successful implementation of ZBB. This is the most difficult part of the ZBB process and is almost always what takes the most time to implement successfully. It's for this reason that many companies choose to implement ZBB in cycles of three or five years, rather than repeating the process annually. Until everyone has adapted to the new way of viewing cost management and company culture, the ZBB process will take a great deal of time and resources to implement. However, as your company begins to shift toward the ZBB mindset, you will begin to notice significant increases in productivity, profits, and customer satisfaction.

I hope that this book has given you insight into how zero-basing can be used to transform your company. For too many companies, growth and success often bring about unforeseen complications, additions, and costs. These new pieces are piled onto the old foundations, until the entire company collapses under its own weight. If you feel like your company is heading in this direction, then you are in luck. You now have the tools you need to reinvigorate your company for the better. Financial planning and prioritizing costs will no longer feel nightmarishly difficult. Hidden costs or unnecessary expenditures will no longer leech money away from your more productive areas. Talented people will feel valued and encouraged to contribute to the company. Digital transformation will catapult your company well into the 21st century, allowing space for technologies that will transform your productivity.

The bigger your company, the more daunting and difficult it will be to implement zero-basing in the beginning. Don't let this discourage you. What seems radical, uncomfortable, and counterintuitive will soon seem perfectly normal. Once you and your team begin to see the benefits of the zero-based method at work in your company, it will become much easier to implement the zero-based principle to all areas of company management. You will find your company capitalizing on market realities that cripple your competition, and seeing just as much benefit from the reinvestment of savings as you do from outright profit increases. Debt will become far easier to manage, and future loans will be taken out with more care than they ever were in the past.

However, before you can begin changing mindsets within your company, you must first adopt the zero-based mindset yourself. Before you begin working with your team to start implementing zero-basing into your budget, there are a few simple questions that you need to ask yourself.

1. **What are my goals?**

You can't prioritize costs to meet company goals if you don't know what those goals are. While it's great to have long-term visions for success, it's also important to set goals that are measurable and attainable. "Increase revenue" or "decrease costs" aren't clear enough goals. More importantly, they don't speak to how you want your company to interface with customers, or what kinds of talent you want to promote within the workplace.

2. **How can I accomplish this goal?**

When you star zero-basing, you'll be pleasantly surprised at how many new ideas your team brings to the table. However, it's important to get the conversation started with some ideas of your own. What are some ways that you can adjust costs, efficiency, or resource allocation? How do these adjustments serve your goal? Train yourself to evaluate how every single decision will promote financial growth and serve the broader goals of the company. Once you've adopted this mindset within yourself, it will be much easier for you to pass that mindset on to other members of your team.

3. **What actionable steps can I take to accomplish my goals?**

The answers to question two are inevitably vague. Things like "install a digital transformation program" or "merge sales and marketing into one department" are the typical answers. Now take a second look at those solutions and break them down into actionable steps. In order to digitize your company, what's the first practical step that needs to be taken? What will that step cost, and how can that cost be worked into the budget?

4. **What are my priorities?**

Always understand which goals are most important to you, as these goals are the ones that need to be funded first. In the example above, decide which goal is most important – digital transformation or merging sales and marketing. When you start zero-basing with your team, make sure that the most important goal is discussed first. Only when that goal is appropriately funded should you move on to the goal that is less important to you.

Answering these four questions will help focus you on the

zero-based mindset. These questions will get you thinking about your company expenses and structures in a zero-based way. Thinking in a zero-based way means thinking in practical and actionable ways. Instead of asking "why is this problem happening?" you'll start asking "how can we solve this problem?" Instead of thinking of spending increases in terms of percentages, you'll start thinking of spending increases in terms of individual functions. Embrace these changes! Thinking in this new way will help you to see how your company runs with far more clarity than you've ever had before.

REFERENCES

Bragg, Steven M. Budgeting: A Comprehensive Guide. Accounting Tools, 2011.

Cheek, Logan M. Zero-Base Budgeting Comes of Age: What It Is and What It Takes to Make It Work. AMACOM, 1977.

Lalli, William R., ed. Handbook of Budgeting. 6th ed. Wiley, 2012.
Pyhrr, Peter A. Zero-Base Budgeting: A Practical Management Tool for Evaluating Expenses. John Wiley & Sons, 1977.

Francisco Souza Homem de Mello, The 3G Way: An introduction to the management style of the trio who's taken over some of the most important icons of American capitalism: Ajax Books; 1 edition (August 14, 2014).

Peter A. Pyhrr, Zero-Base Budgeting: A Practical Management Tool for Evaluating Expenses (Wiley Series on Systems and Controls for Financial Management): Wiley; 99 edition (January 26, 1973).

H. Dean McKay, Business Words You Should Know: From accelerated Depreciation to Zero-based Budgeting - Learn the Lingo for Any Field: Adams Media (January 1, 2008).

Ramit Sethi, I Will Teach You to Be Rich, Second Edition: No Guilt. No Excuses. No BS. Just a 6-Week Program That Works: Workman Publishing Company; Revised edition (May 14, 2019).

Rick Davis, Dan Griffiths, Elevating Trust In Local Government: The power of community-based strategic planning: 978-1-944141-37-0 (May 11, 2018).

Erik Estrada, Understanding Nonprofit Law and Finance: Forty-Eight Key Principles for Philanthropic Leaders 1st Edition: Rowman & Littlefield Publishers; 1 edition (August 13, 2019).

Harvard Business Review, Harvard Business Review on Rebuilding Your Business Model: June 15, 2011.

Blakely-Gray, R. (2017, August 3). What Is Zero-Based Budgeting? | Process and Examples.

Callaghan, S. (2014). Five myths (and realities) about zero-based budgeting.

Correa, C. (2013). *Dream Big*. Brazil: Primeira Pessoa.

Cruze, R. (2019, September 13). How to Make a Zero-Based Budget.

Kagan, J. (2019, April 8). Zero-Based Budgeting (ZBB).

Schwahn, L. (2019, September 7). What Is Zero-Based Budgeting?

The Zero-based Budget (Zbb), Accelerator Of The Digital Transformation? | Banking & Insurance. (2017).

What is Zero Based Budgeting? Learn the basics, steps & more. (2019, August 8).

Zero-based budgeting then and now: Technology remakes the ZBB rules. (2017).

Made in the USA
Middletown, DE
21 January 2022

59334597R00035